THIS BOOK BELONGS TO

____

Intentionally Left blank

NIGERIA

Intentionally Left blank

TANZANIA
AKILI NI MALI
Mount Kilimanjaro

Intentionally Left blank

Located on the Equator

Intentionally Left blank

(C) Elizabeth Abidemi
Akinlabi

Liberian harp, traditional musical instrument

Intentionally Left blank

(C) Elizabeth Abidemi
Akinlabi

ETHIOPIA

Jabena, traditional Ethiopian jug used during coffee ceremonies

Intentionally Left blank

Côte d'Ivoire

Number 1 cocoa producer in the world

Intentionally Left blank

Cameroon

Nkeng (Double Gong) Traditional musical instrument

Intentionally Left blank

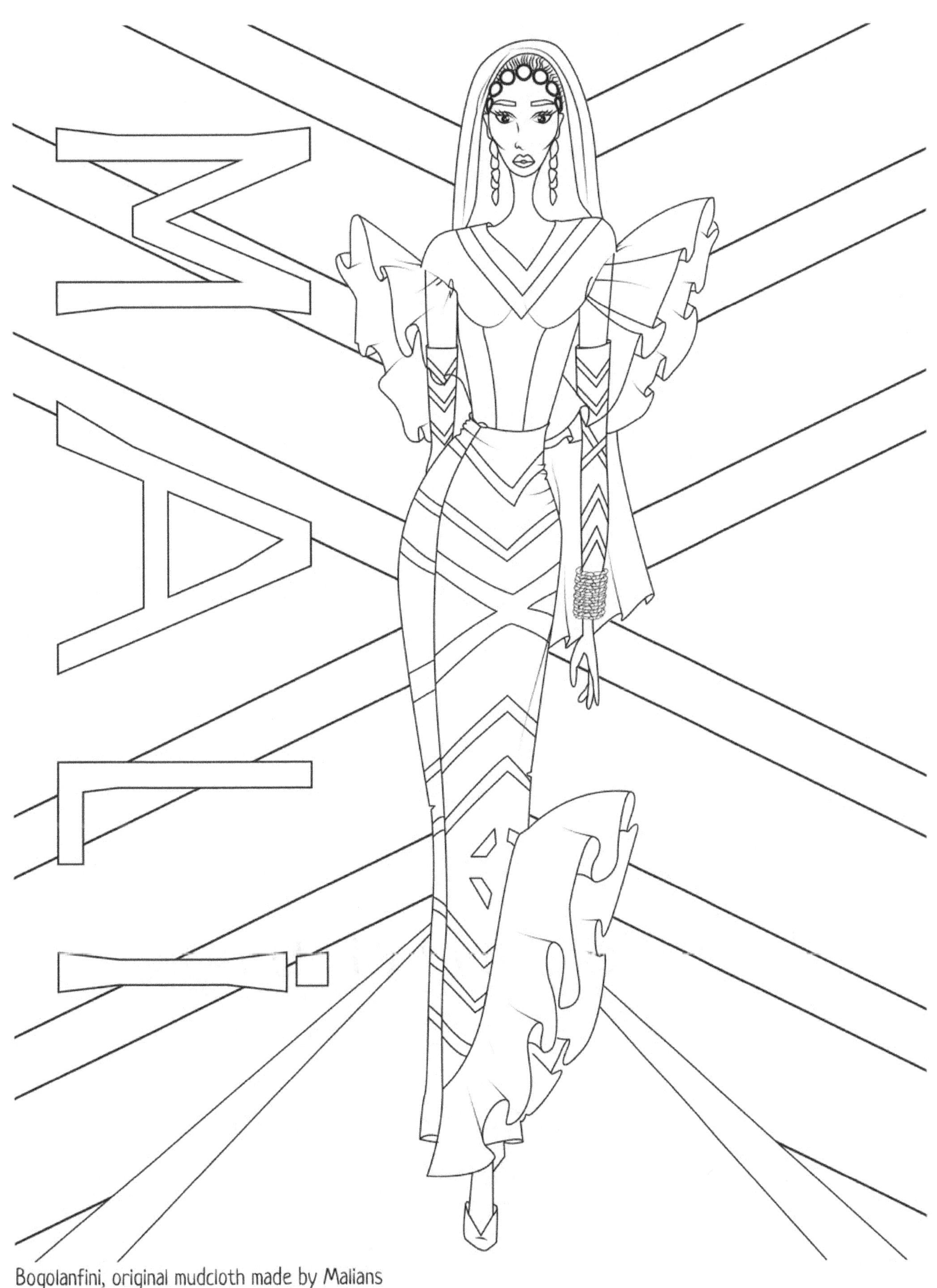

Bogolanfini, original mudcloth made by Malians

Intentionally Left blank

Mozambique

Inspired by the Tsonga tribe

Intentionally Left blank

Egypt

Land of the pyramids

Intentionally Left blank

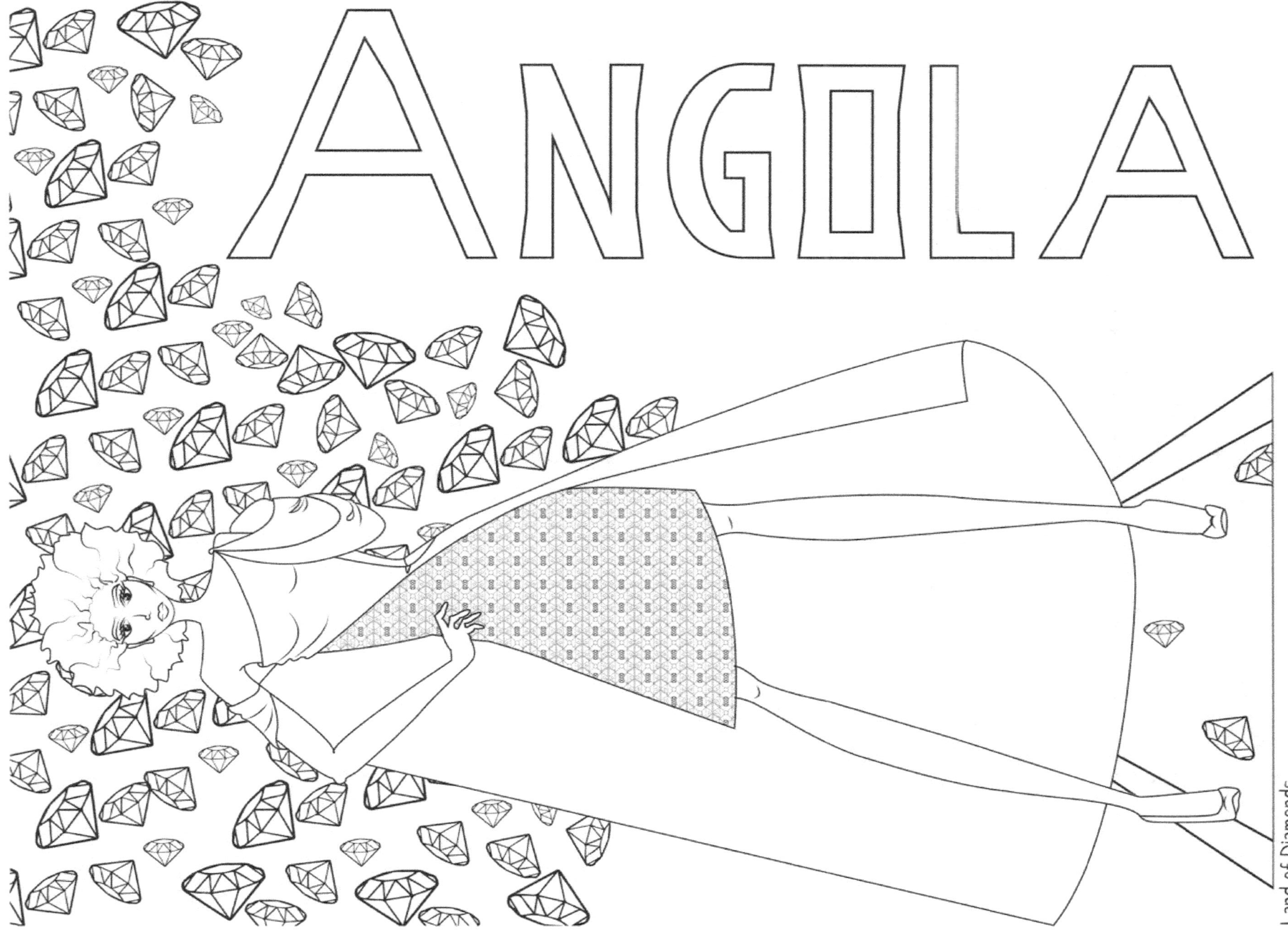

Land of Diamonds

Intentionally Left blank

Inspired by traditional wedding attire of a Madinka bride

Intentionally Left blank

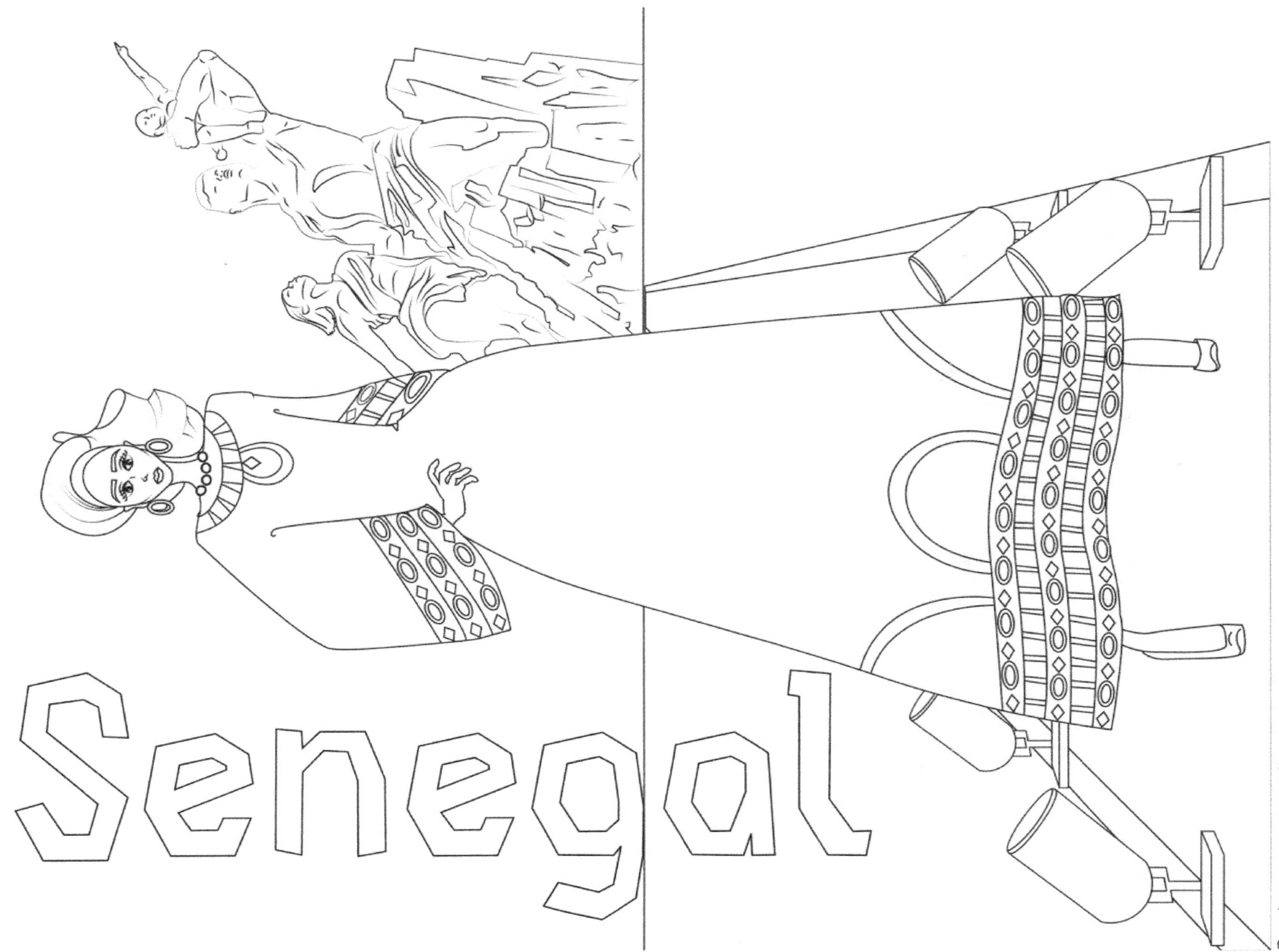

Senegal

Renaissance monument

Intentionally Left blank

Gabon

Fang drum, traditional musical instrument

Intentionally Left blank

Sierra Leone

Kpokpo, country cloth made in in Sierra Leone for over a century

Intentionally Left blank

ZIMBABWE

Mother and child rock formation

Intentionally Left blank

Namibia

Inspired by the Herero tribe of Namibia

Intentionally Left blank

Monument in the Uhuru garden

Intentionally Left blank

Morocco

Bendir, traditional musical instrument

Intentionally Left blank

SOUTH AFRICA

Uhadi, a traditional Xhosa musical Instrument

Intentionally Left blank